"Mother Loyola's name **is an endorsement of every b** **careful use of Mother Loyola's ,. .... best results."** —Rosary Magazine, November 1901

About Mother Mary Loyola:

Most Catholics today who have heard the name Mother Mary Loyola know her as the author of *The King of the Golden City*, which has enjoyed a resurgence in popularity in recent years. But few know that she wrote over two dozen works, and that she was once a household name among Catholics of her era. What made her unique among Catholic authors was her ability to draw in her listeners with story after story—and not just any stories, but ones that incorporated current events and brand new inventions of the time. Despite the fact that those events are no longer current, and those inventions no longer brand new, her books scintillate with the appeal of an active mind that could find a moral in the most unusual places. And while the printed word lacks the animated facial expressions and vocal inflections which reveal a gifted storyteller, hers convey her enthusiasm so capably that the reader can easily imagine sitting at the feet of this wise old nun.

About *First Confession*:

The greatest challenge in preparing young children for the sacrament of Penance is in making confession a habit to which they will be voluntarily attracted. We can require their presence at catechism class, and compel them to go to confession, but without this crucial ingredient, we cannot hope to dispel the all-too-common view that it is an onerous task to be studiously avoided.

It is precisely this difficulty that Mother Mary Loyola addresses with this book. She knew children's minds so well—that they crave being treated like adults—and thus she avoids the temptation to simplify or sweeten the truth, a quality which gives all of her work such broad appeal, even to adults. Her vivid storytelling brings to life an irresistible feeling of the comfort and joy the child will find in the forgiveness of their loving father. Who, then, would dream of ever avoiding such sweet medicine?

To learn more about Mother Mary Loyola, visit our website at **www.staugustineacademypress.com.**

FIRST CONFESSION

A First Confession

First Confession

BY

Mother Mary Loyola
OF THE BAR CONVENT, YORK

EDITED BY

Reverend Herbert Thurston, S.J.

2011

ST. AUGUSTINE ACADEMY PRESS
LISLE, ILLINOIS

This book is newly typeset based on the 1902 edition published by Benziger Brothers. All editing strictly limited to the correction of errors in the original text, the addition of selected footnotes, and minor clarifications in punctuation or phrasing. Any remaining oddities of spelling or phrasing are as found in the original.

Nihil Obstat:

SYDNEY F. SMITH. S.J.,

CENSOR DEPUTATUS.

Imprimatur:

HERBERTUS CARD. VAUGHAN,

ARCHIEP. WESTMON.

This book was originally published in 1901 by the Catholic Truth Society. This edition ©2011 by St. Augustine Academy Press. All editing by Lisa Bergman.

ISBN: 978-1-936639-07-6
Library of Congress Control Number: 2011944130

To The Keepers

of the

Little Ones,

The Holy Angel Guardians,

Who Always See

The Face of their Father Who is in Heaven.

Contents

Preface xiii

To Young Teachers 1

What we must do when our souls are sick . . . 13

Original Sin and Actual Sin 22

Two Sacraments by which Sin is forgiven . . . 23

Getting ready for Confession 28

The Four Things 30

In the Confessional 52

Thanksgiving after Confession 54

Appendix: Updated form for Confession . . . 60

Editor's Note

In reprinting Mother Mary Loyola's *First Confession,* I have done my best to be faithful to the original text as found in the 1902 edition by Benziger Brothers. However, I have, in a few cases, judiciously corrected punctuation, spelling and certain awkward turns of phrase where the change significantly enhanced the clarity of the passage. Therefore the reader should understand that, though this text is considered revised due to these facts, the rest of the material found herein is exactly as it was written over 100 years ago.

One change I did feel was necessary in order to make this book as useful as possible for contemporary readers was to update the form for Confession as given in the book. At the time this book was written, the average Mass-goer was at least passingly familiar with the *Confiteor.* This is the prayer that Mother Mary Loyola has used in her instructions. Today, few are familiar with this prayer, and it has been replaced in the confessional by the Act of Contrition. However, rather than replacing the original version, I have simply added the updated form for Confession in an appendix at the end of the book. In this way, it is easy to access for use in the Confessional.

It is my hope that by reprinting this book, today's children may come to love the Sacrament of Penance and the grace that it brings to our lives, rather than fearing or dreading it. I can think of few people as well-suited for helping to instill this love as Mother Mary Loyola, whose insight and ability to engage the reader is matched only by her solid moral teaching. I hope you will agree.

In Christ,
Lisa Bergman
St. Augustine Academy Press
October 2010

PREFACE

WITHOUT pretending to speak from extensive personal experience, I will nevertheless hazard the remark that there is no portion of his parochial work with which a priest is so often dissatisfied as with the first confessions of the children in his poor schools. Whether the conclusion should be drawn that it would be wise to defer the reception of the Sacrament of Penance until a more advanced age than that usually fixed upon, I do not pretend to decide, but it seems to be the feeling of many persons competent to judge, that the preparation for this important act demands all the careful attention that can possibly be given to it. The danger is that children may come to make their first confessions without understanding sufficiently what they are doing or why they are doing it; and although this want of knowledge may relieve us of anxiety as to any real profanation of the sacrament—an anxiety which in the case of First Communion is by no means chimerical—it is nevertheless likely to initiate a thoroughly bad method. It is hard to shake off a habit once formed, and if a child's early confessions are made as a mere mechanical ceremony, a rite as mysterious to him as vaccination and almost as passive, it is possible that the conscience may go on for years without ever being awakened to the true meaning of the act or the dispositions required for it. Perhaps more real thought goes on in children's brains than we are apt to give them credit for, but after an afternoon spent in hearing first confessions, one has sometimes a recollection of dazed little faces peering up at the priest through the grating of this unfamiliar cage, of tongue-tied silence at the simplest questions, or of heads turned again and again to the door behind them whenever any chance sound outside suggested the possibility of release— marks of nervousness or inattention which, however natural in little folk, often tired out by long waiting for their turn, are not in themselves consoling or encouraging.

I consider, then, that Mother Loyola has never before rendered a truer service to the children to whom she consecrates her talents than she has done in composing this little book. It is a gift of which mothers and teachers and priests will all largely reap the advantage. She cannot indeed impart to *nous autres* those admirable gifts of simplicity, picturesqueness, and apt illustration which are hers by nature, but she has done a great deal in providing a method and in showing the way. There is many a teacher, I venture to predict, who, having in times past been much dissatisfied with her ill success in preparing children for confession, will find a new courage and a new confidence come to her with the acquisition of this book, and will judge that now to be easy which before seemed, of all tasks, the most difficult.

Probably much of the fruit of a first confession depends upon the tact and sympathy of the priest who hears it. In reading this little volume, one is tempted to wish that not only mothers and teachers, but we confessors also, had someone equally familiar with child nature to instruct us how the inevitable strangeness and nervousness of this formidable interview can best be lightened for the youthful penitent. It is eminently desirable that an ordeal which children often dread so much beforehand should leave behind it a pleasant memory of shyness overcome, sin forgiven, and happiness restored; and I feel sure that many of Mother Loyola's priestly readers would be far from resenting any practical advice in this matter which came from a trusted source. Let me conclude, then, by expressing a wish that some priest of experience who has mastered this delicate problem of the right tone in dealing with the souls of very young children may some day be induced to put his impressions on record for the use of those of us who are less happily gifted.

HERBERT THURSTON, S.J.

Feast of the Sacred Heart,
June 14th, 1901.

To Young Teachers[1]

FOR the majority of Catholic children, First Confession is the earliest epoch in their conscious spiritual life. For all, it is the earliest regularly constituted epoch after Baptism. From the period when responsibility begins with the first dawnings of reason, to the time when reason's sufficient development makes the child capable of mortal sin, the conscience is gradually forming under the action of grace and of the various influences brought to bear upon it in home and school life. At length, the Church bids it call itself to account, review the short past, and see how far it has neglected her charge given at Baptism to keep its white robe unstained.

1   The first idea that presented itself in connection with a preparation for First Confession was a book that should serve alike the needs of our young teachers and of the little ones they have to instruct, by providing in the simplest language a sufficient explanation of the Sacrament of Penance. It was a book to be placed in the hands of the children themselves, one consequently from which all notions and words beyond the reach of a child of seven should be rigorously excluded. This idea soon proved impracticable, the extremely narrow limits imposed defeating the end in view. Nothing, therefore, remained but to aim at a preparation as simple as possible which might be put into the hands of children able to use it, and be of some practical use to teachers in dealing with others too young or too backward to read for themselves. The immediate preparation, however, consisting of prayers and short instructions, is easy enough to be placed in the hands of very young children. This is also printed separately at 1d., and may be had from the publishers of this volume.

We have to help here, and because there is question of dealing with the mind and heart of a child, we must bring to our work reverence as well as diligence. For it is no rough and ready handling that is called for, but one delicate and discriminating. We need the gentle tact of the Guardian Angels, who may well envy us a task in which the glory of God and the salvation of souls committed to their charge is closely concerned, a task that is not a duty only but a privilege. For, surely, to this work in behalf of the little ones thus starting on their course, the words attributed to St. Denis the Areopagite, apply in their fulness: "Of all divine things the most divine is to co-operate with God in the salvation of souls."

With regard to the matter of our instructions we cannot surely do better than develop, as simply as possible, the four things the Catechism tells us we have to do when preparing for confession. This is the necessary preparation of the youngest child, and to take the points in order is to accustom children from the outset to an easy, because methodical, preparation. We must bear in mind throughout that there is no question of saying all that might be said, but of selecting and carefully adapting to the mind of a child what is essential.

When we come to the examination of conscience, we are on somewhat slippery ground, and must be careful and discreet. Though the confession of mortal sins alone is of obligation, we shall do well not to lay too much stress on this, but encourage the children to tell whatever sins they remember. It may suffice to explain briefly the few points set down in the examination of conscience that follows. Pass quickly over the Sixth Commandment, taking care not to bring before their minds anything even suggestive of evil. Be satisfied with showing what has to be done in case there should be trouble in any direction. To say sufficient for the needs of all, yet not too much for any one in particular, is perhaps a difficulty. Our safest plan is to get the children to have confidence in the priest, who, because he is in the place of our Lord, will always be kind and comforting. Say we should tell him without fear if anything makes us feel unhappy. He knows all about people's troubles, and will help us and make us happy again directly.

On this point a mother says: "I tell the children that if there is anything they don't quite know how to mention—anything that they think is queer, difficult to explain, or hard to tell—they are not to mind how queer it seems, but to tell it all straight out, even if they are not quite sure that it is wrong; it is better to tell too much than too little. And I add that they are not to think the priest has never heard anything so queer before. He knows all about everything that has been done and confessed ever since the world began, and nothing that they can tell will surprise him. I emphasize this point because I myself suffered agonies, as a child, thinking no one had ever heard such indescribable things as I had thought; and it was a great grace from God that I did not conceal anything. The reason why, in preparing my children for first confession, I departed from the instruction of many priests not to touch upon the Sixth Commandment 'because of the Christian instinct on the point,' was that I found two young nursemaids in my service had spoken to the children of forbidden things. The elder ones told me and added that they were terribly embarrassed about telling it in confession. What the servants said, I do not know, I did not ask. But in preparing the children for their next confession I put before them as strongly as I could, that nothing they could say would astonish the priest. This experience convinced me more and more of the need there is to look after the little ignorant girls sometimes employed in nurseries. Even rather decent girls are sometimes coarse-minded. They see and hear things in their little cottage homes that our children are sheltered from, and they will amuse themselves by enlightening their charges. What was said in this case may not have been very bad, but it was something 'too awfully queer to tell,' and it gave the children a good deal of anxiety."

We must ask the Holy Spirit to put the right words on our lips when we come to this subject, or it may happen that in seeking to avoid one rock we fall upon another. A child warned of the sacrilege of hiding a mortal sin through shame, might, through a false conscience, be led to commit a sacrilege by hiding what was no sin at all. It may associate natural shame with sin. Take an opportunity of saying that not everything we are ashamed of is a sin. We may blush crimson for having said something that makes us look silly, yet there was nothing wrong in what we are so ashamed of. And there is never anything wrong in what we cannot help. But if we think something was a sin, or if we are unhappy about something, we should tell the priest we are in trouble and he will put it all right for us.

Difficulty comes sometimes from the particular priest to whom we go to confession. Tell children that, should this happen, we are not obliged to make known to the confessor that what we say concerns himself.

An acolyte of the Church of St. Mary of the Angels, Bayswater, used to tell how he went to confession one evening to Dr. Manning, at that time in charge of the mission, and how, on entering the confessional, he found it impossible to begin. In vain did he try again and again to bring out what was on his mind. In vain did his confessor seek to encourage him by saying he must have heard many a time the thing that was troubling him. His penitent was sure he had not. At last with a violent effort the poor boy blurted out: "I called you Daddy long-legs!"

When preparing for confession most of us, perhaps, have to guard against the tendency to give an undue proportion of time to the examination of conscience. If children are taught to classify their duties, and to know what come under the headings: (a) to God; (b) to our neighbours, and (c) to ourselves, they will not need much time to make the review of their short lives. They have really been occupied with examination of conscience, whilst you have been talking about children's faults in general, as you may gather at times from an approving nod when you happen to strike home, or from a counting off of fingers, or a nudge to a neighbour. The interest they invariably take in the misdoings of other children, can be utilised, after Nathan's fashion, in any direction and to any extent. Tell them stories which, by bringing out certain faults, will make self-examination easy. Ten minutes when they are actually preparing for confession should be enough. It is a great mistake to tire them with a long examination. Keep their minds fresh for what is of far greater importance—sorrow for sin. Their good angels surely implore us to be merciful and *reasonable* here. What can we expect from a poor little creature whom we send into the confessional thoroughly tired out!

Try to arrange that children shall not have long to wait for their turn. Wait with them, and when they are ready, find them some prayers to say, or some pictures to look at, *e.g.*, the Stations of the Cross.

As to the motives for sorrow and purpose of amendment, experience seems to show that it is better to dwell on one or two, than to suggest many. Different motives can be taken at different times. Get them to notice which appeal to them most strongly, and advise them to go to that oftenest when preparing for confession. The mother quoted above says:

"I have found that the Agony in the Garden is the best subject to give as a reason for being sorry. The children easily understand our Lord's horror when the load of our sins was thrown on to His white Soul. It was as if some immense heap of unmentionable refuse were thrown upon one of us. They can understand how His horror and disgust were so overwhelming, that they cast Him down upon His face on the ground and forced the drops of blood from Him…And we remember that, being God, He could distinguish in that load the share of each of us, as if it were the only one; that He felt the weight of it and the dirt of it quite distinctly, and that it helped to crush Him down."

This little book being offered to teachers merely by way of suggestion, and on the supposition that they will introduce anything further that in particular cases may seem advisable, these hints may suffice perhaps as to the *matter* of our instruction. With regard to the method, we must all be agreed that in dealing with little children, so sensitive to outward impressions and so helpless in our hands, the utmost attention must be given to our *manner*.

The idea of providing a book to be read by very young children was abandoned the more readily from the conviction that, do what we will, they cannot be got to read. Even the stimulus provided by the picture on the opposite page of their reading-book, fails to act after a minute or two of application. Nay, they do not like us to read to them: "*Tell* us about it," is their constant pleading. It is the necessity of meeting this need that makes attention to our manner of giving instruction so imperative. Our eyes, our expression, the tone of our voice, our way of speaking, animated or otherwise—this is the book in which they read, whether we will or no.

It is most important that a child's first experience of spiritual things should be a happy one, that it should be drawn not driven. Some of us, perhaps, can remember instructions before confession that were anything but fascinating. The help given us did not take an attractive form, or leave in our minds anything pleasant in connection with the great sacrament which is the stay of our spiritual life. Could we not, in these days of child-study, do something to make preparation for confession less of a dreaded task than we ourselves may have found it?

In order to do this, we are bound to recognize the limitations that meet us on every side when we are dealing with the opening mind of a child. To expect mature growths, from what is only in germ, is foolish, not to say cruel. Nature has an invaluable lesson for us here. We must imitate her slowness and self-restraint, and so act that every influence tends, like hers, towards the end in view. Our words, our manner, our smile, the tone of our voice, should be like the harmonizing action of sun, and rain, and quiet-lying dew upon the opening buds. Her angry moods are quite the exception—a flash of lightning now and again—all the rest gentle, imperceptible working, yet covering the earth with verdure and golden harvests to the end of time.

Seeing how needful it is to repeat the same thing again and again, it is fortunate for us that the child-mind does not resent such repetition. Quite the contrary. A few simple truths, with plenty of varied illustration, is a food taken with relish and better suited to it than an abundance which it cannot digest and assimilate.

Illustration is simply indispensable. Its concreteness arouses the child's interest and calls forth its remarks. These furnish a clue to its mind and enable us to discover how far we have made ourselves understood. Only get a child to talk, and everything else will follow. How ingenious children can be in misunderstanding our plainest directions, those know who have had experience in this particular matter of preparing them for confession.

"Remember to ask the priest's blessing when you go in; say the first part of the *Confiteor*, and then begin to tell your sins: 'I accuse myself of so and so, and so and so,' " was a teacher's final word to the two dozen little creatures gathered round the confessional. Next time the confessor met her he observed drily: "I wish you would teach those children how to go to confession. The whole set of them started with 'I accuse myself of *so and so, and so and so.*' "

Acting on the injunction not to name a third person in confession, one child began: "In the name of the Father, and of the Son, and of the——Amen." Another thought he had done wrong in saying he had disobeyed his mother. We cannot be too simple in our use of words and phrases, or too careful to ascertain that our meaning has been grasped.

Could we recall the instructions of our early days, we should probably find that not one tenth of what we heard made any lasting impression, and nothing whatever that served to interest. The lesson of this is obvious. We *must* interest. We must come down to the level of the little ones. We must watch their opening faculties, see with their eyes, hear with their ears, look out with them upon a world all new and strange, and bring within the reach of their perceptions as much of abstract truth as they can take in—and no more. "*I gave you milk and not meat for you were not able as yet,*" says the tender, motherly heart of the great Apostle (1 Cor. 3).

No good will be done unless the children follow us with pleasure. If you see attention flagging, have recourse at once to illustration. Seize hold of anything coming to hand that enters within the sphere of their experience or interest. They love animals; weave in some curious story of a dog or a monkey that you have in reserve, and that with a little stretching may be made to bear upon your subject. We should always have our eyes open and our tentacles feeling about for anything that will add to our store of illustration. Or you may fall back upon their games or some little event that has made a stir in home or school life and is uppermost in their thoughts at the moment. Inattention shows you have lost touch with their mind. You must catch some vehicle to bring you up with it again. Do not blame them for wandering after something more interesting than you are, but make yourself so interesting that there is no temptation to wander. And be short. Ten minutes or a quarter of an hour at a time is as long as we can expect to fix the thoughts of little children on such subjects as we have to drive home. Beware lest by length or by heaviness, by regarding their instructions as a lesson that has to be learnt, or by exacting too much of them, you create weariness and disgust, and thus lose all the fruit you hope for.

We must be very patient and content with little, bearing in mind, not merely the weakness of the child's powers, only just beginning to exert themselves, but also the abstract nature of the matters in which we are seeking to interest it. In these days of Kindergarten training, everything is brought within the range of the child's experience; it must see, and handle, hear, or taste all it is expected to know. From a natural point of view, therefore, we are at a tremendous disadvantage, and have to make use of all expedients our ingenuity can devise to arrest the attention and secure interest for our subject. At the same time, we must beware of overeagerness, and of expecting to see much in the way of results. If our lesson is well thought out and brightened with familiar illustrations, more will sink in than we are aware of, and for the very reason that it sinks in, it will not appear just yet. We must remember, too, that a child cannot take stock of its impressions. These are hazy at first, and need to be renewed and strengthened by experience before it is definitely conscious of them and can give expression to them in words. Like Mother Earth, we have to work on in the dark, *patiently waiting for the precious fruit* (St. James 5) that will not fail to show itself in season.

I.

What we must do when our souls are sick.

CATHOLIC children ought to have bright faces. The sunshine in their hearts should make their faces glad. Why? Not because they are better off in this world than others. Many of them hardly get enough to eat, and their clothes are very poor. Besides, we know that good things to eat and drink and fine clothes cannot make any one really happy. What is the reason, then?

Wise people who understand these things tell us that one reason is this: Catholic children know how to get their sins forgiven. It is sin that makes us dull and unhappy. Not at first, perhaps. When we have done what was wrong to please ourselves, we are glad for a little while, but it is only a little while. Then we begin to be dull and sad. And if we often do what we know to be wrong, our heart gets so dull that the dulness spreads over our face. Sin is like those green sweets that are nice just whilst we have them in our mouth. But they leave a bad taste and pain behind, and we wish we had never touched them.

Many little Protestant children do not know what to do when they have done wrong. They are told that God will forgive them if they are sorry. But they do not know if they have been sorry enough, or how to make themselves really sorry. They want to know God has forgiven them. They would like Him to tell them that He has.

A Protestant child used to lie awake sometimes in her little bed and wish God would call her as He called the child Samuel, that she too might say: "Speak, Lord, for Thy servant heareth." When she grew up she became a Catholic. Would you like to know why even as a child she wished to be one? She shall tell us herself.

"My sister and I had several little friends of our own age with whom we used to play in Merrion Square, Dublin. Some were Catholics and some were Protestants, and we were strictly forbidden to speak to the Catholics on religion. One of our play-fellows was a little girl named Kathleen, who lived quite close to us. In the summer evenings we used to be allowed to play in the square until nine. I remember Kathleen coming laughing and dancing up to us one Saturday evening. Seeing me looking at her in surprise, for she was unusually merry, she said, 'Oh, I do feel so happy, I've got rid of all my sins.'

"'Whatever do you mean, Kathleen?' I asked.

"'Why, I've been to confession, and all my sins have been forgiven,' she answered. And then she went skipping off somewhere and I had no time to ask what she meant. But the words remained in my mind; I often thought about them and wondered what they could mean, and I date my wish to be a Catholic from that evening in the square."

Of her school life, she tells us: "Though I was good at my lessons, I was very troublesome in other ways. I used to talk at study-time, light the gas after it was put out at night, and do many other things which were forbidden. Sometimes, as a punishment, I was made to get up at night, dress, and go downstairs, and sit in the cold schoolroom writing pages of history or geography. But this only made me more naughty. Still, in my heart I often wished I were good and obedient, and I used to say to myself, 'If I were only a Catholic I could get my sins forgiven, and start afresh; but now I can't, and I am out of friends with God; so I suppose unless I become a Catholic I must go to hell.' "

This poor child did not know how to set about being better—how to get her sins forgiven. And so it is with many little Protestants. They wish they could go to their Heavenly Father as they go to their father and mother here on earth when they have been naughty, and put it all right and begin again.

Can a Catholic child do this? Yes. It knows quite well what it must do to get its sins forgiven. No wonder, then, that little Catholics look bright. They know that they sometimes displease their Father Who is in Heaven. But they know, too, that He is very kind—kinder than the kindest father they ever heard of, and that He will always forgive them if they want to be forgiven. They know that when they have told His priest what they have done, and have been really sorry, the priest, who is in God's place, will forgive them their sins. It will be just the same as if they heard our Blessed Saviour say to them: "Thy sins are forgiven thee—go and now sin no more." Oh, how happy a Catholic child ought to be!

A little boy named Jeff was very fond of horses. His greatest delight was to go to the stable and feed and pet them. Now, one of the horses, the black one, was not a safe animal to pet. He could not be trusted. When he seemed most friendly, he would suddenly turn round and bite, or strike out with his hoofs and hurt any one who happened to be near. So Jeff was told to give up patting and petting this dangerous play-fellow and to keep out of the stable. His father, a doctor, knew what a terrible thing a kick might be, and it was because he loved his little Jeff dearly that he forbade him to do what would hurt him.

Did the boy do as he was told? No. After a time he began to peep into the stable; then he went just inside; and at last, when no one was looking, he would go in and play with the horse as before. "I wonder why father forbade me," he said. "Raven has never kicked me yet and he never will. I am not afraid. I will not go too near. No harm will come."

One afternoon, the doctor left home to visit a poor woman who lived just across the fields. He had not been in the cottage five minutes when an old servant, all out of breath, came in. "Oh, sir, come home at once. Master Jeff has been into the stable and Raven has kicked him. He is lying in his mother's arms in a dead faint." The father hurried home and into the yard. There, by the stable door, was a little sad crowd—brothers, and sisters, and servants, round the boy who lay in his mother's lap—face and hair covered with blood that kept trickling from a deep gash in the forehead. His father carried him upstairs and laid him on his bed. When he came out of the room he looked very grave.

"The boy's head is badly hurt," he said, "and he must be kept very quiet. I shall send for a hospital nurse; no one else must go near him." The brothers looked sad and the sisters began to cry.

"Will he get better, father?" they asked.

"Yes, if he takes my medicine and does just as I tell him. I will put some ointment on the cuts and bruises to take away the pain and make them heal."

For many days Jeff lay in bed all in the dark. No one, I think, would have known him, except perhaps his mother— his face was so swollen and ugly, black and blue with bruises. He saw the sunshine trying to come in through the blinds. He heard his brothers and sisters in the garden laughing and shouting at their play, and he wondered if ever he would be in the garden and play in the sunshine again. But he had learned a good lesson. He did as he was told now. And when his father brought to his bedside the ointment that was to make the sore places well, he let him put it on without a word. Poor little Jeff! He did so want to be well again.

And he did get well. One by one, the ugly marks the black horse had made went away, and his little face looked as it was before. It was a good thing for him that his father had the precious ointment ready. Without that, he might have died, you know.

Now let us think of another Father, another sick child, and another sickness— a great deal worse than Jeff's.

The good Father Who forbids His child to do what would hurt him—is *God*. The sickness that comes of disobedience—is *sin*. The child who hurts himself by disobeying his Father—is *myself*. But what is it that is to make me well again? That I must find out.

Jeff's father was very kind. He did not scold his little sick child, but brought him something to make him well. So does our Heavenly Father. He has a precious ointment ready for our sore souls—oh, how precious it is! It cost Him a great deal to get it. It was got on Good Friday, when our Lord died on the Cross. It is the Precious Blood of Jesus.

I wonder if you can guess what the black thing is that will hurt us if it can? It is the devil. We must not go near him. We must do as our Father tells us and keep away from him. The devil tries to make us tell lies, to laugh and talk in church, to get into tempers, to quarrel, to pout and sulk when we cannot get our own way. If we do these things, we go near him. We shall be hurt, and the ugly marks of sin will come on to our souls.

If you get a looking-glass when you have the measles, you will see how ugly you look. When our souls are sick, they are covered with ugly spots that would frighten us if we could see them. God sees, and our Guardian Angels see, how we have spoilt ourselves. We do not put spots on our faces. But we put ugly marks on our souls. Can we take them off again? No. Only God can do this.

Let us see how it is that our souls become sick, and how sin spoils what God made so beautiful.

It is hard to understand what sin is, because it is so very bad and dreadful. It is the most dreadful of all things, worse than pain, or any harm that can come to us—God's little creatures—because it is harm done to the great God Who made us. You would say it were better for any hurt to happen to a wasp, than that you should be hurt by its sting. And it would be better for any harm to happen to us than that the great God should be offended. If we do offend Him, we must expect punishment, just as we expect to be punished if we disobey our parents. How much punishment, depends on the badness of the fault. If your father told you not to meddle with his papers, and you did, you would be severely punished, because this was a big fault. If he told you not to tease the cat, and you disobeyed, you would deserve punishment, but not much, because the fault was small. So it is with disobedience to our Heavenly Father. He has given us His Ten Commandments, which tell us not to kill, not to steal, not to speak ill of our neighbour, and so forth. When we do these things, we commit sin by disobeying Him, and we have to be punished, more or less, according to the greatness of the sin.

The punishment it deserves helps us to understand what a dreadful thing sin is. All the pains that come to us in this world are the punishment of sin—hunger and thirst, heat, cold, toothache, the trouble it is to learn our lessons. And the far harder troubles we see around us and hear about—blindness, deafness, sickness of every sort; the sorrows of the poor, all the suffering caused by plague, famine, fire, storms by sea and by land, earthquakes lightning, war. And what comes to every one of us—death. All this is the punishment of sin. Whether the pain comes to good people or bad, sin is the cause of it all.

More still: The pains of this life are very many and very terrible, but they are nothing to the pains of the next life in hell or in purgatory, caused, every one of them, by sin. Oh, what a dreadful thing that must be that brings so many dreadful things upon us! Must we not hate sin above all other evils? Thank God if He has put into your heart the fear of offending Him by sin. He could not give you a surer sign that He loves you dearly and wants you to come safely to Him in heaven, where the ugliness of sin is never seen, where all are full of joy because they can never sin any more.

You must not think that the fear of sin will make you dull or sad. Not at all. It is sin, not the fear of it, that makes people gloomy and cross. No saint perhaps hated and feared sin more than St. Philip Neri. "Only let there be no sin," he used to say. Yet there never was a merrier saint than this dear old man. He could not bear to see people look upset or glumpy, and the funny things he used to say and do would make you laugh.

God cannot help punishing sin, because He is just. The very big sins—called mortal—deserve a punishment that will never end. They are called mortal or deadly, because they kill the soul by taking away the grace of God, which is its life.

The snakes we find in our fields do not kill by their bite. But in India, there are serpents whose fangs or teeth have poison in them. When these fangs bite any one, the poison is squeezed into the wound and kills a man in a few minutes. Are you glad that we have none of these dangerous creatures in this country? Stop a moment. There is a serpent that can get at us even in England. It does not lie hidden in the long grass and dart out upon us as we pass, and kill the body. But if we are careless and are not afraid of it, it will bite the soul with its poisonous fangs and *our souls will die.* The name of this serpent is *mortal sin.* God Himself tells us it "bites like a serpent." He tells us to keep out of its way all our life long. When we are little and when we grow up we must always be afraid of it. It can never bite us unless we want to be bitten. We must ask God to make us afraid of it and not to let it come near our souls. The way it comes near is this: we say to ourselves, "I will tell mother I did not spill ink on the carpet. Nobody saw me do it and I shall not be found out. A lie is not a mortal sin, it won't matter much." And we tell that lie. Another day we take three figs out of Jack's hamper, saying to ourselves, "He will not miss them, and taking three figs is only a venial sin, it doesn't matter much."

Now these words, "It is only a venial sin, it doesn't matter," are very dangerous and we must never say them. If I get careless about little sins, I shall get careless about big ones too. Some day the devil will put a big temptation in my way. I shall say, "This is a mortal sin." But as I have never said "no" to myself in little temptations, I shall not say "no" then. I shall do that mortal sin and—*my soul will die!*

I knew a boy named Alfred. He had a good father and mother, and he was sent to a good school. There, after a time, he began to take little things that were not his—cakes, toffee, a few pence lying about—always saying it was not much, only a venial sin. When he left school, he was sent to an office, and there, one day, he took a large sum of money. He said to himself he meant to pay it back, but it was very wrong and he knew it. His theft was found out and he was sent to prison. The judge said it should be for one month only, as it was his first offence, and he hoped it would teach him a lesson. Think how his poor mother cried at the thought of her boy being sent to prison as a thief! At last he was let out, and a kind friend took him into his own office to give him another trial. For a time, all went well. Then he began to thieve again, a little at a time. At last a very large sum of money came into his hands, and he ran away with it. But he was caught and sent to prison again for a long, long while—for many years. When he came out, no one would have anything to do with him, and he had to leave his father and mother, and brothers and sisters, and go to a far off country without money, without friends, or any one to love and care for him. This came from letting himself do little sins and saying, "*It doesn't matter.*" And all this harm done to his body was nothing to the harm done to his soul by that sin. Stealing a large sum is a mortal or deadly sin and kills the soul.

Venial sin does not kill the soul, yet it displeases God and often leads to mortal sin. It is not a small thing because it is smaller than mortal. Next to mortal, venial sin is the most dreadful thing in the world. I may not steal a penny to give it to a poor man. Because to steal is a venial sin, and all sin is an offence against God.

God hates all sin. It makes our souls look ugly in His sight, just as a face covered with a rash looks ugly to us. There is a terrible disease called leprosy, which so disfigures the body as to make it horrible to look at. No one who has seen a leper would say that his disease does not matter much. It makes his life very wretched, and if it does not kill at once, it leads to death.

When our Blessed Saviour was on earth, He was kind and tender to all the poor sick who were brought to Him to be cured. St. Luke says that "laying His hands on every one of them, He healed them." Yet it was noticed that to poor lepers He showed Himself more gentle, more pitying than to any others. Why was this? Perhaps because leprosy is a figure of sin—that is—it is like sin. It wounds, it spoils and weakens the body, and puts it in danger of death. All these things sin does to the soul. Now, our Lord cares more for our souls than for our bodies. If, then, He made such haste to cure poor lepers that came to Him, never keeping them waiting a minute, laying His blessed hands softly on their horrible wounds that no one else would touch or even look at, how glad He will be to take away the leprosy of our souls. We must see how He does this.

Original Sin and Actual Sin.

There were different kinds of leprosy, and there are different kinds of sin—two kinds, the Catechism tells us, original and actual. Original means the beginning. The sin in the Garden of Eden is called original because it was the first sin committed in the world, the beginning of all the rest. Original sin is not our own sin but Adam's. It comes to us because we are his children, just as disgrace belongs to children whose father has been a traitor to his king. Every baby is born with original sin on its soul, and unless that sin is washed away, it can never go to heaven and see God. Our Lord died for us on the Cross that it might be washed away. The Precious Blood He shed for us there has opened heaven to us. But the good that comes to us from His Precious Blood must be applied to us—that is—put on to our souls in some way. How is this done?

Come into the garden, and you will see. All the water in the world is of no use to your pansies and pinks unless it is applied to them. Your can is full, yet for all that, the poor thirsty things may droop and die. But you hold the can over them, and through the holes in the rose, tiny showers of water fall upon them, and they lift up their little heads and drink it in, and suck it up with their roots, and by it live and grow. Something like this happens to our souls. The Precious Blood of Jesus stored up in the Church flows down upon them in the seven streams of the Sacraments. It refreshes them when they are tired. It comforts them when they are sad. If they are sick it heals them, and—this is more a great deal than the water does for your flowers—if they die, it raises them to life again. How we ought to thank our Lord for giving us these wonderful Sacraments! To receive them worthily must indeed be the greatest happiness in the world.

Two Sacraments by which Sin is forgiven.

Have you ever been in church when a baby was being baptized? Oh, if we could only see what God and His holy angels see before and after the water is poured! They see a poor little child of Adam brought to the font with a dark stain on its soul that keeps it out of heaven. A few minutes after, when the water has been poured and the words have been said, they see the happy little thing carried away a child of God and heir of heaven. Into that water, and into those words, God put His almighty power to wash away the stain from its soul. Now that soul is bright and beautiful in His sight. It has a right to heaven, it is heir to a throne, and if it dies now, without sin of its own, it will go to its throne straight and see God for ever.

But notice this—before the little child is taken away from the font the priest says some very solemn, words to it: "Receive this white garment and see thou carry it without stain before the judgment-seat of Christ." Now suppose the child, when it grows up, commits mortal sin and loses the beautiful robe of grace it got at Baptism—what is it to do? Can that white robe be got back? Yes, because God is good. He will give it back, but not so easily as He gave it at first. Original sin was not the baby's own sin, and so God took it away without the baby doing anything on its part. But if, when it comes to know what sin is, it commits actual sin—sin that is its own act—it will have to do something to get that sin forgiven.

Before the Church would give us baptism and make us children of God, she made us promise to renounce, that is, to fight against God's enemy, the devil, and to keep God's law, the Ten Commandments. As we could not do this for ourselves, our godfather and godmother did it for us. But the promise is really *ours*, for the Catechism says *we* promise to renounce the devil and all his works and pomps. As we grow up, we are bound to keep this promise. If we break it, we displease God, and must do what He tells us to do before we can get forgiven. What it is that He tells us, we are going to see now.

We can never be baptized again, but our Lord has made another sacrament for the forgiveness of sins. This is the Sacrament of Penance, "whereby the sins, whether mortal or venial, which we have committed after Baptism, are forgiven." How kind it was of Him to do this! He might have said to us at Baptism: "I forgive you original sin, because that was not your fault. But if by your own fault you commit sin, I cannot forgive you any more." But He did not say this. He knows how weak we are and how strong the devil is who tempts us. And so if we do commit sin, He has pity on us and tells us to come back to Him and He will forgive us again—again and again, as often as we want to be forgiven. Oh, how good God is to us!

When did our Lord make this comforting sacrament? Not on that sad Thursday, the day before He suffered, when He made the sacraments of the Holy Eucharist and Holy Orders. But on Easter Day, the brightest and gladdest of all days, when from early morn till night He was going about, rejoicing the hearts of His friends. "When it was late that same day, and the doors were shut where the disciples were gathered together, Jesus came and stood in the midst and said to them: Peace be to you…Whose sins you shall forgive, they are forgiven them." (St. John 20.) By these words He gave to them, the first priests of His Church, and to all priests who were to come after them, power to forgive sin.

He loved to forgive sin when He was living here on earth. He loved to say these words: "Thy sins are forgiven thee." He loved to be in the midst of poor sinners, just as a doctor likes to be in the midst of his sick. When people wondered to see sinners all about Him, He said that those who are in health do not need the doctor, but those that are ill.

But what was He to do when He went back to heaven? Poor sinners would want Him still. We should all want to hear Him say to us, "Thy sins are forgiven thee." He could not bear to see our souls ugly with sin and our faces sad. So He gave His priests the same power that He had Himself. We are to go to them as we would have gone to Him. He has promised to forgive what they forgive. When the priest in the confessional says, "I absolve thee from thy sins in the name of the Father, and of the Son, and of the Holy Ghost," God really forgives what His priest forgives—if we have done our part.

What, then, must we do when our souls are sick? Just what we do when our bodies are ill. We go to the doctor. We tell him what is the matter with us, and he gives us something to make us well again. Some people are so uneasy when they feel a little poorly, they are so afraid they may get worse and perhaps die, that they go off at once to the doctor and tell him all about it and beg him to give them some medicine directly. "Please, give me some medicine," they say. "I don't mind how nasty it is, I will drink it." See what care people take of their bodies, these poor bodies that have to die some day! Must we take less care of our souls?

Our Blessed Lord calls Himself the Doctor of our souls, and He says we are to come to Him when they are sick. Until children are old enough to know what God's Commandments are—what He tells them to do and not to do—they cannot commit sin by disobeying Him. But a child soon learns what is right and wrong, and about the age of seven, it perhaps knows enough to do that dreadful kind of sin which is called mortal because it kills the soul and deserves hell.

So at seven or thereabouts it has to go to confession. Not, mind, because it has mortal sins to tell, but because it very likely has venial sins and it *might* have mortal. Many, many children have only venial sins to confess. However this may be, all, about the age of seven, have to prepare for their first confession. Our Lord bids them all come to Him to have their sins forgiven.

And we ought to be glad to go. The sea-gulls we used to watch last summer were always dipping into the waves. There were no dusty roads to soil their feet, but only the rocks along the beach on which they rested from time to time—the clean, tide-washed rocks. Yet the beautiful creatures were never tired of bathing. They cannot bear the least speck on their whiteness. We must be like them and try to keep our souls always pure and beautiful in the sight of God Who made them for Himself. We came from the waters of holy Baptism like the white birds from the ocean, without spot or stain. But before we went away the priest said to us these solemn words: "See thou carry thy white garment unstained before the judgment-seat of Christ." The priest spoke for the Church. But how can the Church expect us to go through a long life without ever staining our white robe by sin? She does not expect it, nor does God expect it. What she means is this: See you do not come before God to be judged with the frightful stain of mortal sin on your soul, and do not be careless about little sins or you will come to do big ones. Even if you are careful you will soil your robe sometimes, and you must come to the Sacrament of Penance to get the stain taken off.

There was once a little girl who was afraid to go to confession. She did not like to be told she would have to go some day, and she used to think what she could do to get off going. One day she said to her mother: "I have found out a way not to go to confession. Now I am too little, and when I get bigger I won't do the things." But she found that when she got bigger she did do the things, not the same things perhaps, but others. And so, when she was seven years old and had more sense, she was glad to go and get all these things washed away in the Precious Blood. And when she grew up to be a woman, and when she was an old grandmother, she never missed going to confession at the right times. And sometimes she would tell her little grandchildren how silly she had been when she was quite little, and laugh to think how she tried to keep away from the sacrament our Lord has been so kind as to make for us.

II.

Getting ready for Confession.

OUR BLESSED LORD loved to be with children. He loved to sit on a green slope and watch them at their play. He looked so kind that they would often leave their game and gather round Him, trying who could get nearest to Him. The little ones wanted Him to take them on His knee. The bigger ones wanted Him to put His arm round them and lay His hand on their heads. They would talk all together and tell Him all their news—that their goat was dead—that they had a new frock—that mother was ill at home—that they were hungry—that they had fallen and hurt themselves. Other things too—that they had been disobedient—that they took some figs when no one was looking, and they were afraid of being found out and punished. They looked straight up into His face and told Him all the truth. They knew He would not be angry whatever they said.

Turn to the picture at the beginning of this book. See where that little child is kneeling and Whose arm is round him. He has done some naughty things, but he is sorry, and wants to be good and not do the naughty things any more. He has found our Lord quite alone. And our Lord has called him by his name, and taken him on His knee, and said to him: "Now come and tell Me all about it." See, he is not afraid. He is glad to be there quite by himself with Jesus. What he has done I cannot tell you. No one will ever know. It is a secret between himself and Jesus. He knows our Lord will not tell. He knows He will be kind and forgive him. See how he makes his first confession. He does not look about. He joins his hands. He tells our Blessed Lord just what he has done. And Jesus listens and says he is a good child to have told Him all so bravely. And He forgives him and sends him away quite happy.

You would like to have been that little child. You would like to make your first confession to our Lord Himself. He would help you to say all you have to say, and then He would lay His hand on your head and forgive you everything, and tell you to run away and be happy, and He would not think of the naughty things any more.

Well, you *are* going to Him now. It is true you will not see or hear Him. You will kneel down at the feet of His priest. But He will be in the tabernacle close by and will hear all you say. You will be as near to Him as the little child in the picture, and He will say as He puts His arms round you and draws you to His side: "Come now and tell Me all about it!" He is very kind, and He has told His priest, who is in His place, that he must be kind too. So the priest will not scold you, no matter what you say. Our Lord never tells any one what we say to Him. And the priest will not tell. So there is nothing to be afraid of.

Our Lord knows you want to make a good confession and He is going to make it quite easy. It is because He wants to make it easy that He bids you tell your sins to a priest. He might have told you to kneel down before a great grand angel. But you would not have dared perhaps to tell him, who had never done wrong, the things you have done. You will not be afraid of a priest, who has to go to confession himself and who knows how hard it is sometimes to be good. He will not be surprised at anything you say. Many other children have told him the same sins that you have to tell. Think you are kneeling at the feet of Jesus and you will not be afraid.

The Four Things.

The Catechism says we have four things to do to get ourselves ready for confession: first, we must heartily pray for grace to make a good confession; secondly, we must carefully examine our conscience; thirdly, we must take time and care to make a good act of contrition; and fourthly, we must resolve, by the grace of God, to renounce our sins, and to begin a new life for the future.

I.
I must ask God to help me to make a good confession.

You see, He does not do all by Himself. He is very glad to help us, but we must do our part. He is looking at you now, to see if you want Him to help you. Tell Him you want it very much.

My God, You know I want to make a good confession. And You know too that I cannot do anything good by myself. Please help me. Help me to find out my sins, and to tell them to the priest. Help me to be sorry for them. Help me not to do them again.

Dear Mother Mary, pray for me and help me.

Dear Angel, ever at my side, even when I was naughty, help me to remember the naughty things you saw me do and that made you sad.

My dear Patron Saint, ask Jesus to make me sorry for my sins.

II.
I must carefully examine my conscience.

We cannot tell our sins in confession till we have found them out. Now, some of us can find out other people's faults much quicker than our own. We see what our brother or sister has done, and do not see what we have done ourselves. I will tell you about some children I know. You will soon see what their faults are. Think if you have any of those faults, and if you have done any of the things they did, or things of the same kind. If you have, remember to tell them when you go to confession.

Freddie is a greedy child, always wanting nice things to eat. The best things at table he tries to get for himself. And outside of mealtimes you will see him munching and sucking, as if he could not be happy without something in his mouth. Whenever he sees anything good to eat, he thinks how he can get it. All his pennies go to buy tarts or sweets—none find their way into the poor-box. He does not give what he buys to anyone else, but eats it all by himself. Sometimes he takes so much cake or pudding because it is nice, that he makes himself sick—Am I greedy?

I hope you are not like Philip. If anything teases or vexes him—if the strap of his skates breaks, or his mother says "No" when he asks to go on the river with some other boys, he gets into a passion, calls things by ugly names, is rude to his mother, and behaves worse than a little wild beast. No one likes to go near him when he is in one of his tempers. I have even known him to throw himself down on the ground and kick. None of the servants, not even his mother, could get him to move. It was well for Philip that he had a father who was very firm; and who made him ask pardon of the servants and kneel and beg his mother's blessing before he would forgive him.

And yet, do you know, I would rather have Philip with his temper than his sister, little Miss Minnie, with her sulks. If her mother says anything she does not like; if she cannot be "captain" when the children are playing at robbers, she pouts and goes out of the game. For the rest of the day she is quite cross, and, what is worse, she tries to pay the child back who was made "captain." She goes and tells tales of her just to get her into trouble—Oh, I do hope you are not like Minnie!

Arthur is Philip's cousin. He is something like him but not quite like. He is a quarrelsome boy. He thinks every one ought to give in to him at play, and when his brothers and sisters will not do this, he quarrels with them. One of his brothers is nearly as quarrelsome as Arthur, and it is sad to see the two together. Of course both cannot have the best bat, or the warmest place by the fire in winter, or the nicest story-book, or the first ride on the bicycle when school is over. And instead of thinking of what the other wants and being kind and giving in, each thinks only of what he wants himself, and so they quarrel about little things all day long—Am I like them?

Alice is an idle girl. When her mother wakes her in the morning and tells her it is time to get up, she says: "Oh, do let me stay in bed a little longer. I am so tired. I am poorly. My head aches." She dawdles over dressing, grumbling all the time and saying how sleepy she is. When she kneels down to say her prayers, she does not kneel up straight, but lolls upon the bed or a chair. She goes down to breakfast with her face and hands half washed and hair all untidy. There she sits leaning back in her chair half asleep whilst her brothers and sisters are as fresh as larks. When they are ready to start for school, they have to leave her behind. She cannot find her books or her slate, because instead of putting them in their places, she throws them here and there. At last you will see her creeping along to school like a snail. Of course, she often gets into trouble for being late, and because she has been too lazy to do her home lessons, she has to stay indoors when the others are all out at play. Then she thinks she is very badly treated, every one is very unkind, her lessons are too hard or too long. If you go into the class-room you will find her crying over a blotted copy-book or sums that will not come right. Even on a holiday she will not play about like her brothers and sisters or even sit up to read a book, but lies about on the grass doing nothing, just like the sleepy cows. The cows lie down because they cannot sit up, and sleep because they cannot read or play. But Alice—is there any excuse for her? Is she really tired or poorly? Not a bit. She is cross, and a dunce, no use to any one at home or at school, not because she is weary, but because she is lazy—Am I like her?

What a giddy thing a butterfly is! Now on one flower, now on another, never still for a moment. Kitty is like that—never still, not even at her prayers. As soon as she kneels down, her head turns here and there, her eyes look about everywhere. She does not make the Sign of the Cross and try to think that God sees her and is waiting to hear what she has to say to Him. He loves little children very much. He loves Kitty, and He knows that her little head turns about this way and that because she is like a butterfly. He knows little children forget, and that all kinds of things come into their heads. But He knows, too, that when they kneel down they can make the Sign of the Cross nicely, they can begin to say their prayers, and when they find out that they are thinking about their play, or their rabbit, or their new frock, they can try not to think of it then. They can look at the altar and watch the priest, or they can look at the pictures in their prayer-book. But their eyes should not wander all round the room or the church—Do mine do this when I kneel down to pray?

I wish you could see Rose when she is looking in the glass. You would laugh. She turns her head this way and that, and smiles at herself. "What pretty blue eyes I've got," she says, "and what nice hair, all yellow just like my dolly's. And I've a much better frock and hat than Annie Frump; her mother is poor and she can't have nice things like I have. I am much nicer than Annie. I shall show her my new frock on Sunday, and she will wish she had one too." Rose is vain. I wonder if Almighty God thinks she is much nicer than poor little Annie. Pretty eyes and nice hair do not make a beautiful soul—I should not like to be Rose.

I know a little boy called Hugh. He is not old enough yet to go to confession, but he tells his mother he wants to go, "Because," he says, "I have many sins to tell, mostly disobediences." Some of us are like little Hugh. The sins we find out are "mostly disobediences."

And now I want to tell you about Max. Poor Max! he used to be such a truthful boy. But when he found that boys at his school got off punishment by telling stories, he thought: "Why should I tell the truth and be punished?" One day some fine pears had been taken from the garden; Max had helped to take them, but he said to himself: "I will say I never went near the tree; it will only be a venial sin." And he told this lie and many more afterwards. Let us see what happened at last. He had spoilt a very beautiful book belonging to his father by leaving it out in the rain. As he had been told not to touch that book, he was afraid of being punished for his disobedience as well as for his carelessness. When his father asked who had taken the book from his room he said he had seen a servant reading it under a tree. The poor girl was sent away. This lie was not a venial sin. Oh, why did Max keep saying when he told untruths: "It is only a venial sin"? Did he not know that venial sins lead to mortal? But you will be glad to hear he was very sorry when he found that an innocent girl had been punished for his fault, and though he knew his father would be very angry, he went bravely to him and said: "Father, I took the book. Do let Kate come back." From that day Max began to mend. He did not get better all at once. Sometimes he said what was not true, through the bad habit he had, or for fear of being punished. But little by little, he got the good habit of telling the truth, because he asked God to help him, and because he was so afraid of telling a big lie again. And at last he came to be so truthful that every one trusted him—Have you ever been like Max?

Do not think that only boys have the faults of Freddie, Philip, Arthur, or Max, and only girls are like Kitty, and Alice, and little vain Rose. Oh no, there are plenty of greedy, quarrelsome, disobedient girls, and plenty of idle boys. You know what the children I have been talking about will have to say when they go to confession, and if you are like them, you know what *you* will have to say. But it is all mixed up in your mind. You must try to make it clear or you will forget it.

Read slowly what is coming, and when you get to the full stops…put your finger on them *and stop*. Think if you have done that sin, and once, or often.

- Have I missed saying my morning and night prayers . . . ? Have I said them in a hurry and without thinking of what I was doing, looking about all the time . . . ? Have I done this sometimes or very often . . . ?
- Do I examine my conscience at night prayers to see what faults I have done in the day . . . ? Do I say my grace before and after meals as I ought . . . ?

- Have I used bad words . . . ? Once, or twice, or often . . .?

- Have I behaved badly in church by talking or laughing . . . ? Have I made others behave badly . . . ? Have I said my prayers carelessly at Mass . . . ?

- Have I disobeyed my parents, or any one else whom I ought to obey . . . ? Have I done what I was told at once . . . ? Or been angry and answered back . . . ? Or been sulky . . . ? How often have I done these things . . . ?

- Have I been in a passion . . . ? Have I struck any one or quarrelled . . . ? Sometimes, or very often . . . ? Have I given bad example . . . ?

- Have I done by myself anything I feared was very wrong? Anything which would have made me turn crimson with shame if my father or mother had found me doing it . . . ? Once, or many times . . . ?

- Have I got others to do what was wrong . . . ? Have I said naughty words, or taught them to any one else . . . ? How often . . . ?

- Have I thought of naughty things on purpose . . . ? (If I tried not to think of them, there was no harm.)

- Have I taken or kept anything that was not mine . . . ? Have I kept my school-money or spent it . . . ? Once, twice, or often . . . ? (If I can I must give back what I have taken, or ask the priest what to do.)

- Have I told lies . . . ? Have I told lies against any one . . . ? Once, twice, or very often . . . ? (If the lie has done harm to others I must tell the person I told, that what I said was not true.)

- Have I been greedy . . . ? Have I eaten meat on Friday . . . ? Once, or often . . . ?

- Have I stayed away from school . . . ?

- Have I gone with bad companions . . . ?

- Have I done anything else that I ought to tell . . . ? (It will help me to remember my sins if I think of the houses I have lived in, and the rooms in them—the children I have lived with or played with—the way I spent my time there, at lessons, or at play.)

If you feel afraid to say anything you ought to say, or if you do not know how to say it, tell the priest this when you begin your confession. He will help you, and you will be happy directly. But never leave a big sin out or tell a lie about it because you are afraid. Remember, the priest will never be angry with you, and he will never tell. If you have tried to examine your conscience properly and still forget a sin, it will be forgiven with the rest, even if it is a big one. Only it must be told when you remember it, because every big sin must be confessed. But if you hid a big sin because you were afraid, God would be very angry with you. You would not get any of your sins forgiven; you would be very miserable; and next time you went to confession you would have to tell that sin, and that you had hidden it. Else, it would be told to the whole world at the Last Day. So never leave out anything you think you ought to tell, anything that makes you unhappy. Say: "Father, help me to tell my sins because I am afraid."

III.
I must take time and care to make a good act of contrition.

Remember this—God will not forgive any sin, not even a very little one, unless you are sorry. Suppose you said to your father: "I have been disobedient, but I don't care, and I don't mind if I do it again," would he forgive you? Of course not. Would you expect him to forgive you, even if he was very kind? No, you would not. And you must not expect God to forgive you unless you are sorry. He could not do it. God can do all things. But not even God can forgive us our sins unless we are sorry for them. If you have big sins to confess, you must be sorry for every one of them. If you have no big ones, you must be sorry for one at least of the smaller sins which you confess.

Some children think it is hard to get sorrow for their sins. Let us see if it is hard. Suppose your father wanted very much to give you a knife and promised you should have it if you asked for it nicely. And you did ask—very nicely. Would that knife be hard to get?

You want sorrow for your sins. God can give it, and He wants to give it. Will it be hard to get? Surely not. If you want to be sorry, and ask to be sorry, you *will* be sorry.

Sorrow is the chief thing we want when we go to confession. But see what some children do. They think of everything else but this. They count up all their sins, and put them together into little heaps that they may not forget any. They really do take care to examine their conscience. And then they go straight off to confession. Silly little things! It is like a baker going to make bread—getting his oven ready, and his water, and his salt—and forgetting all about the flour!

If we were to ask some children: "How many things have you to do to prepare for confession?" I think they would have to answer: Four things:

1st, I must carefully examine my conscience.

2nd, I must carefully examine my conscience.

3rd, I must carefully examine my conscience.

4th, I must carefully examine my conscience.

For this is all they do. They do not even ask God to help them—the first thing. When they get into church, they set to work at the second, and when their turn for confession comes, they are at it still. No time and care for the good act of contrition. No good resolution to be better children after their confession. They never think of the two last things. And yet sorrow for what we have done, and a good resolution not to do it again, are the chief things we want. We *must have them* before we go into the confessional. A horse must have his four legs to go anywhere. He cannot get along with one, or even with two or three. Neither can we do without these four things. All four must be ready to take us to confession whenever we go. And they will not be ready of themselves. We must get them ready.

Sorrow for our sins is called contrition. How are we to get contrition? The Catechism tells us: "We may obtain a hearty sorrow for our sins by earnestly praying for it, and by making use of such considerations as may lead us to it."

We will pray earnestly for it now.

Dear Jesus, I can do wrong by myself—but I cannot be sorry by myself and make myself good again. Please help me. Make me very sorry for all I have done to displease You.

Making use of such considerations as lead us to sorrow, means thinking of things that will make us sorry. *Thinking,* mind. If you will not take the trouble to think, you do not really mean to be sorry. You are like a little boy who asked his mother to show him a picture. And when she got the book down and turned to the page—he would not look!

It will make us sorry for our sins to think what sin is. Sin is an offence against God. If it were only a king of this world whom we offend by sin, it would not matter so much. *But it is God.* He is so holy that the Saints fall down on their faces before Him and the Angels cover their faces with their wings. All the bright worlds you see about you at night, and all the men and women in this world of ours are like a few grains of sand to Him—He is so great. And He is so good, that if we could spend all our life in loving and praising Him, it would not be half as much as He deserves. Think what it must be to offend a God like this—to be disobedient to Him—to do what we know He has forbidden.

My God, it must be a dreadful thing to offend You. Make me afraid of sin. Make me sorry for my sins.

It will make us sorry for our sins to think how sin spoils the things God has made. Sin changed the beautiful angels into ugly devils. Changed them in a minute. And sin changes our souls too. Mortal sin makes a soul that was beautiful before, quite ugly.

A mother was sitting under a tree in a sunny field. It was a big field with a high hedge all round, except where, just in front of her at the bottom of the hill, the gate opened out upon the railroad. She was reading, but now and again laid down her book to watch the fair-haired child sitting among the buttercups and daisies, or listen to its merry laugh as it trotted after the butterflies. Lost at last in her book, she turned page after page till the shrill whistle of the train roused her and she looked up. She looked up and around, but—where was the boy? Nowhere to be seen? Nowhere? What was that white patch down there outside the gate? What was it? With a cry she started to her feet and dashed down the hill. The child saw her coming and, shouting with glee, ran forward on to the rails. Her hand was on the gate as the train swept past. And then? And then—oh, poor mother! Summoning up all her courage she went on to the line and gathered up—what? I cannot tell you: you could not bear to hear. No trace in what she held in her arms of the bright laughing face that had looked up into hers a moment ago—nay, scarcely a trace of face at all.

What a dreadful story! you say, but is it true? Quite true. And a thousand times less dreadful than what happens when sin, horrid sin, comes down upon one of God's children—a little soul in the state of grace—and crushes out the life that made it beautiful in His sight. Oh, how we ought to hate and fear sin! Ask our Lord to make you afraid of it.

Dear Jesus, make me afraid of sin. Never let me kill my soul by doing a mortal sin.

It will make us sorry for our sins to remember that we shall have to be punished for them. Those who die in mortal sin are punished for ever in hell. This punishment will never come to an end—never. Those who die without mortal sin on their soul, but who have done venial sins—who have behaved badly at their prayers, or been disobedient, or got into tempers, or told lies—these will be punished too. They will have to go to purgatory, where the pains are very dreadful and last a long time.

God is obliged to punish sin. He had to punish the Angels, and Adam and Eve. He has to punish every one who commits sin. He will have to punish me. How sorry I am when I have done something I shall be punished for! How I wish I had not done it! How I make up my mind not to do it again! Then I must be sorry for having deserved the terrible punishments of purgatory—a great deal worse than any pains I ever heard of!

O my God, I am sorry—and beg pardon for all my sins—and detest them above all things—because they deserve Your dreadful punishments. Do not punish me as I deserve. Forgive me because I am sorry—and because I will try not to do these sins again.

Something else will make you sorry for your sins. Look at this picture of Jesus on the Cross. One day He was really hanging just like that. If you had been on Mount Calvary, you would have seen Him. Not quite plainly, because it was dark. Have you ever been in pain in the dark, with toothache, or earache? The darkness seemed to make the pain worse. That was why our Lord made it dark that Good Friday when He was on the Cross. He wanted the pain to be as bad as He could bear. How He ached on the Cross—His head, His arms, His hands, His feet! If I try to hold out my arms quite straight, I shall be so tired in three minutes that I shall have to let them drop. His arms were tired, but He could not let them drop because the sharp nails held them fast—for three long hours!

Look at His head pricked with thorns on every side. Look at His poor hands and feet. Oh, how sore they were! If you were to take a pin or even your little soft nails and press them into your hand, you would feel how this hurts. The rough iron nails through His hands and feet were bigger than a man's finger. How they must have hurt Him! He could have taken them out if He liked. He could have come down from the Cross. But He thought of you and of me, and He stayed there for us. We had done the harm and He hung there to suffer instead of us.

We can learn, when we are very small indeed, to be sorry for our Lord's pains.

Before they could speak plain, a mother used to teach her little children to pity Jesus on the Cross. When she had one of them on her lap, she would take a crucifix and lay a little finger gently on each of the five wounds. And the child would say after her: "Poor Jesus, I am sorry because the nail hurt You so in this hand…I am sorry because the nail hurt You so in this foot."

One day when her youngest boy had been repeating after her: "I am sorry for Your pain when the nail went in here," he suddenly turned to her and said: "Why aren't you sorry for His head?" And ever after, a little finger was laid pityingly on the thorny crown with: "And I am sorry for the pain in Your poor head."

Now, if a very young child learned more and more of our Lord's pains by looking thoughtfully at a crucifix, and as he learned more, grew more pitying, would he not also grow in hatred of sin when he came to know it was sin that caused all that bitter pain? Let us do as this baby did. Let us learn to pity Jesus and to hate sin as he learned it.

The feeling for our Lord's pains did not come all at once. It grew little by little. The boy had heard of the scourging, and knew that the cruel wounds it made were still bleeding on the Cross and smarting in the cold wind. One day, his hand went softly round that figure crucified as he said: "And I am sorry for the pain in Your back too." The pains he had found out for himself moved him most. What we find out for ourselves always touches us more than what we hear from others. Is there any pain of Jesus crucified that we can find out for ourselves and soothe with our pity and our love?

Dear Jesus, I am very sorry for my sins because they have hurt You so much. I am sorry most of all for this one (tell Him which). I wish I had never done wrong because it displeases You. Forgive me and help me not to displease You any more.

Many reasons, you see, may make us sorry for what we have done. It need not always be the harm that has come to ourselves. Even a little child may be more sorry for the pain of one it loves than for its own. A child of four had been terribly hurt by putting its hand between the rollers of a mangle. When pitying people came to soothe it with kind words, it held up the poor little crushed fingers and sobbed out: "Mother will cry so."

Do you think you could be more sorry for giving pain to one you love than for hurting yourself?

Suppose your father told you one morning not to go to the house of one of your little friends on your way home from school, because the boy was very ill with small-pox, and if you went near him you might catch that dreadful disease; and he promised that if you were obedient you should go with him at night to see the fireworks on the common. And suppose you were disobedient and went to the house. When night came and you had to go to bed instead of going out, you would be very sorry. You would cry because you had to be punished, because you had lost your treat. The pleasure of having your own way was soon over, and now you were all alone and crying.

And suppose your father heard you crying, and came to you when you were in bed, and said he was sorry too—because you had been unkind—because you had cared more to please yourself than to please him. He thought you loved him more than that, and he was sad. And now he was going out all by himself. He would not enjoy the fireworks, as you were not with him. And he had looked forward to your pleasure for so many weeks, and been counting the days with you.

What would you have done, if you had seen the tears in his eyes? Would you not have sprung up and flung your arms round his neck and sobbed out: "O father dear, I am so sorry, so very sorry—not because I can't see the fireworks, but because I have made you sad. I do love you, indeed I do. Please forgive me and wipe away your tears. I won't go to Bob's house any more if you tell me not."

You would be crying now, not so much for yourself as because you had grieved your kind father and made him lose his treat. Thinking about the punishment of your disobedience made you sorry. And thinking about your father made you sorry too. Which was the better kind of sorrow? Which was it that comforted your father?

Think now of another Father. The sins you have found out were all acts of disobedience to your Father, Who is in heaven. And so you will have to be punished for them, either in this world or in the next. This is something to be sorry for, because the punishment of sin in this world hurts very much, and in the next world it hurts still more. But there is another reason, a better reason still. God has been very good to you. He made you because He wants you to be happy for ever. No one can be with God without being quite happy and having all he wants. God wishes you to be in joy like this—for ever. You hear a boy say, "When the holidays come I'll be as happy as the day is long!" God wants you to be as happy as eternity is long. Why? Because He loves you. He has made a place for you in His beautiful heaven, and He is always thinking how He can make it more beautiful, that you may enjoy it more when the time comes for you to go there. If you were to put together all the treats you can think of, all you would like to have, and like to do, you could not think of anything half so delightful as what God has thought of for you. How you enjoy surprises on your birthday! Well, He has got ready for you surprises that you would never guess. He is longing to see how pleased you will look when you find them out. He has counted the days to those happy holidays when you are to go Home to Him and have all His presents. He longs for the day to come.

And you have been unkind to this kind Father. You have been disobedient to Him. When He told you not to do things that would hurt you and keep you out of heaven, perhaps for a long time—you have done those things. Are you not sorry for grieving God, Who is so good—your Heavenly Father, Who has loved you so dearly?

My God, I am sorry and beg pardon for all my sins— and detest them above all things—because they deserve Your dreadful punishments—but most of all Because they offend Your Infinite Goodness.

My dear Father In heaven, I am sorry for all the naughty things I have done because they have displeased You Who are so good and kind, and because I love You. I do love You, Indeed I do. Please forgive me and help me to be a good child after my confession.

See how many reasons there are why we should be sorry for our sins! We need not think of them all. Choose the one you like best, and think about that. But notice this: the sorrow we get out of them all is a supernatural sorrow. To be sorry for a sin because it has brought disgrace upon me, or punishment, is easy enough. This sorrow may be very real and very strong. But it is quite *natural* and no use for getting the forgiveness of my sins. I must be sorry for some *supernatural*, that is, *more than natural* reason—for some reason that my faith puts before me, such as those I have been thinking about. The best sorrow of all is that which comes from the love of God—to be sorry because God is so good in Himself. God loves to see this sorrow in our hearts. He loves us as soon as He sees it there, no matter what sins we have done. He loves us even before we go to confession. Ask Him often to give you this sorrow. It is called perfect contrition. There is perfect contrition in the act you know by heart; "O my God, I am sorry and beg pardon for all my sins—and detest them above all things—because they deserve

Thy dreadful punishments—because they have crucified my loving Saviour Jesus Christ—*and most of all because they offend Thine Infinite goodness.*"

It often costs a great deal to get the best things—the best toys, the best clothes. But it does not cost much to get the best sorrow. It is not hard to be sorry for grieving those we love. Did your mother ever say to you when you had been naughty, "Go away, I do not want to see you, you are not my little child. We are not friends to-day"? I have seen a sulky, pouting child burst into tears when its mother said that. I have seen it go up to her and try to put its arms round her neck and sob out, "O Mother, I am sorry, be friends with me again."

Perhaps you will think that because God is so great He does not mind when we are out of friends with Him. But He does. He minds very much. And He holds out His arms to us and tells us to come back to Him and He will forgive us.

He was not obliged to forgive sin. He did not forgive the Angels, and they will be out of friends with Him for ever. He forgave Adam and Eve, and He will forgive us if we ask Him as we ought. I must ask Him now, with all my heart, to make me sorry and to forgive me.

My God, do make me sorry for my sins. And make me afraid of sin. What hurts my body does not matter much. But sin that hurts my soul and may make me out of friends with You for ever—this matters.

And now I want to say something which you must try to understand. It happens very often that a child who has tried to make a good act of contrition does not *feel* sorry. And so he thinks he is not sorry. A boy said to a priest: "I know I was sorry when my mother died. I cried all night. But I have never cried for my sins, so I can't be really sorry for them." This boy made a mistake. He *felt* very sorry when he heard of his mother's death, and he cried bitterly. Some saints, like St. Peter, have wept bitterly over their sins. But there can be real sorrow without tears. Sorrow is not in our eyes but in our heart. If we say as well as we can, "I am sorry for what I have done; I wish I had not done it; with God's help I will try not to do it again," we are really sorry.

Notice these last words, "I will try not to do it again." You always say this when you ask your father or mother to forgive you. God expects you to say it to Him, and to mean what you say. He does not expect you will never do any of those things again, but only that you will *try* not to do them. And so the last of the four things we have to see to when we go to confession is a purpose of amendment.

IV.
I must renounce my sins and begin a new life for the future.

What do you do when you have fallen once or twice in the same spot? You look about to find out what it was that made you slip there. Was it a piece of orange-peel? Or had boys been making a slide? Or did you stumble on a stone? You look back to find out what it was, that you may not fall there again.

Look back now. Think of the chief faults you are going to confess. In what places did you make those slips? Was it in church? Or in the schoolroom? Or in the playground with a companion? Think how you can prevent falling again in that place. Say to yourself, "What is the worst thing I am going to tell in confession?" or "What have I done oftenest? And what must I do to be better?"

If I say my prayers carelessly in church or at home, looking about all the time, I will remember when I kneel down that God is looking at me to see how I am going to speak to Him. When thoughts of play or other things come, I will try to send them away as soon as I notice them.

If I do wrong by going with a companion who does wrong, I will ask the priest what I must do.

Pick out one fault that you will try most of all not to do again, and say, "With God's help, I will try to be better *in this*. At least I will try not to do it so many times."

"I shall have many sins to tell, *mostly disobediences*," said little Hugh. No doubt when the time comes for his good resolution, he will see how the disobediences can be put an end to. Freddie will try to find a cure for greediness. Philip will take in hand his temper, and Minnie her sulks. And they will all ask God to help them to mend their faults. The quarrelsome brothers will see what they can do to be kind to one another. Alice will say perhaps: "I will jump up the minute I am called, and try to be first at school instead of last." And Rose?—well, I should advise her to hide her looking-glass or put it where she cannot get it, and to think sometimes that if her face is pretty now it will not be pretty in the grave, and that it is silly to think so much about these poor bodies which will be hidden away under the ground some day.

What is *my* resolution to be about? I could advise all these children wisely; I must advise myself. It is better to make a purpose of amendment about one or two things, than about many things. What would our Lord like best? I must talk to Him about this. I shall soon find out what He wants, for He will whisper it gently in my heart. And if I ask Him, He will help me to give Him what He wants. He loves to help, and He is so strong that He can do it quite easily. If a tiny ant asked me to push out of the way a grain of sand that stopped up the road to its home, would this be hard for me? Nothing is hard to God. I will ask Him to put out of my way the fault that stops me from getting on fast to my Home in heaven.

Dear Jesus, You love little children, and You like to help them to be good. You love me and You want to help me. I am very sorry for all the sins I am going to tell in this confession—most of all for this one which I think was the worst. (Tell Him what it is). Forgive me this time—and help me not to do that sin again. I will try not to do it. Put Your arm round me when the devil comes and wants me to do what is wrong. Help me to say "No" to him and to drive him away. Make me afraid of little sins, because If I do little ones I might come to do big ones—and make You very angry with me.

When it is near your time to go to confession, think again what sins you have found out, that you may have them quite ready to tell.

III.

In the Confessional.

1. Kneeling down in the confessional, make the sign of the Cross:

In the name of the Father, and of the Son, and of the Holy Ghost.

2. Ask a blessing:

Pray, Father, give me your blessing for I have sinned.

3. Say the first part of the Confiteor:

I confess to Almighty God, to Blessed Mary ever a Virgin, to Blessed Michael the Archangel, to Blessed John the Baptist, to the holy Apostles, Peter and Paul, to all the Saints, and to you, Father, that I have sinned exceedingly, in thought, word, and deed, through my fault, through my fault, through my most grievous fault.

4. Tell your sins in the way you can remember them best. Say how often or about how often you have done them. At the end, say:

For these and all my other sins which I cannot now remember, I am heartily sorry and humbly beg pardon of God, and penance, and absolution of you, my ghostly Father.

Therefore I beseech the Blessed Mary ever a Virgin, Blessed Michael the Archangel, Blessed John the Baptist, the holy Apostles, Peter and Paul, all the Saints, and you, Father, to pray to the Lord our God for me.

5. When the priest says in Latin the words of absolution:

"I absolve thee from thy sins, in the name of the Father, and of the Son, and of the Holy Ghost. Amen," bow down your head, and say:

My God, I am very sorry for all my sins because You are so good.

6. Listen attentively to what the priest says to you. Do not begin to think if you have forgotten anything. It is not the time for that now. And it is no matter if you have forgotten. There are some children who do not attend to the priest when he is giving them good advice. They are still thinking about their sins and wondering if they have forgotten any. They are doing this even when the priest is giving them absolution. This is silly. They have something much more important to do.

Be sure you hear what penance the priest gives you. If you do not hear, or if you do not know the prayer you are to say, you must tell him.

7. Come out of the confessional, and go to your place with your eyes cast down.

IV.

Thanksgiving after Confession.

WHAT a happy child you are now! All your sins are forgiven. Your soul is all sparkling and beautiful in the sight of God and His holy Angels. Thank Him as well as you can.

My God, I thank You with all my heart for having forgiven me my sins.

Glory be to the Father, and to the Son, and to the Holy Ghost. As it was in the beginning, is now and ever shall be, world without end. Amen.

I thank You with the good thief, and St Peter, and St. Mary Magdalen, and all the saints in heaven whose sins have been forgiven.

Glory be to the Father, and to the Son, and to the Holy Ghost. As it was in the beginning, is now and ever shall be, world without end. Amen.

I thank You with my good Angel, who is so glad to see me now with all my sins forgiven.

Glory be to the Father, and to the Son, and to the Holy Ghost. As it was in the beginning, is now and ever shall be, world without end. Amen.

Think now of what the priest told you to do or not to do. If you have to give back anything you have taken, or to unsay something untrue you said of somebody, see how soon you can do this.

Tell our Lord again what the fault is you are going to fight against and ask Him to help you.

Help me, dear Jesus, to keep my good resolutions, and not to give up trying when I break them sometimes, perhaps very often.

Not to give up—this is the resolution our Lord loves. We shall not mend all at once. Max did not break off his bad habits and become a truthful boy the minute he wanted to be one. He had to try hard, and often he broke his resolution. But he did not give up: "Try, try, try again," he said to himself. This is what we must all do. Will the quarrelsome boys be like two little angels as soon as they come from confession? Not a bit of it. Or Alice be a busy bee directly? No. They will all break their good resolutions many and many a time. But shall I tell you who will succeed in the end? Not those who tried most the first day or two and then gave up. But those who, like Max, go on and on, who are sorry when they break their resolution, and then try again as if they had never broken it. This is very brave. I will do this. I will be like Max.

My God, I will try not to do these things again. Most of all I will try not to do this one (say which). But if I do it again, I will not be cross and miserable, and say it is no use trying. I will say directly: "My God, I am sorry. Forgive me once more." Then I will try again.

The Penance.

This is very short and easy. But if you say it well, it will take away a great deal of the punishment you have deserved by your sins. Say it now as well as you can.

If you like, you may pay a visit to our Lady's altar before leaving the church and put your good resolutions into her keeping:

Dear Mother Mary, remember that I am your child. Jesus gave you to me for my Mother when He was on the Cross, and asked you to love me and take care of me. Please do, and take care of my good resolutions. Help me not to forget them. And help me, Mother dear, to drive the devil away when he tempts me to do what is wrong. Hide me under your blue mantle and keep me safe all my life from mortal sin.

My good angel and my patron saint, help me and pray for me.

If you enjoyed this book, you might want to read some other books that Mother Mary Loyola wrote:

Forgive us our Trespasses is meant to take you from your First Confession to your last, and it is also helpful to others who have not used this book. Everything you need to know before entering the confessional is in it, and there are even stories to read while waiting your turn.

First Communion is usually the next step after you have received the Sacrament of Penance. It is a much larger book than this one, but just as pleasant to read, and it is meant to be read only a little at a time.

The King of the Golden City is a wonderful book to read once you have finished *First Confession* and *First Communion*. It is a story version of what you will learn in these books, and is a very nice way to remember the important parts.

The Little Children's Prayer Book includes simple morning and night prayers, prayers used in the Mass, a complete examination of conscience, and prayers for Benediction as well as before and after Communion.

APPENDIX

Updated form for Confession.

1. Kneeling down in the confessional, make the sign of the Cross:

In the name of the Father, and of the Son, and of the Holy Ghost.

2. Ask a blessing:

Bless me, Father, for I have sinned.

3. Say how long it has been since your last confession:

It has been ___weeks since my last confession. (Or this is my first Confession.)

4. Tell your sins in the way you can remember them best. Say how often or about how often you have done them. If you are nervous or afraid, ask the Priest to help you. At the end say:

For these sins and all the sins of my past life, I am truly and heartily sorry, especially for the sin of (say which sin).

5. Listen attentively to what the priest says to you. Do not begin to think if you have forgotten anything. It is not the time

for that now. And it is no matter if you have forgotten. There are some children who do not attend to the priest when he is giving them good advice. They are still thinking about their sins and wondering if they have forgotten any. They are doing this even when the priest is giving them absolution. This is silly. They have something much more important to do.

Be sure you hear what penance the priest gives you. If you do not hear, or if you do not know the prayer you are to say, you must tell him.

Now recite the Act of Contrition:

O my God, I am heartily sorry for having offended Thee, and I detest all my sins because I dread the loss of heaven and the pains of hell, but most of all, because they have offended Thee, my God, who are all good and deserving of all my love. I firmly resolve, with the help of Thy grace, to confess my sins, to do penance, and to amend my life. Amen.

6. When the priest says the words of absolution:

"I absolve thee from thy sins, in the name of the Father, and of the Son, and of the Holy Ghost," bow down your head, make the sign of the Cross and say:

Amen.

7. The priest will dismiss you, saying "Go in peace, your sins are forgiven." Say:

Thank you, Father.

8. Come out of the confessional, and go to your place with your eyes cast down. Say your penance right away.

Additional titles available from

St. Augustine Academy Press

Books for the Traditional Catholic

Titles by Mother Mary Loyola:

Blessed are they that Mourn
Confession and Communion
Coram Sanctissimo (Before the Most Holy)
First Communion
First Confession
Forgive us our Trespasses
Hail! Full of Grace
Heavenwards
Holy Mass/How to Help the Sick and Dying
Home for Good
Jesus of Nazareth: The Story of His Life Written for Children
The Child of God: What comes of our Baptism
The Children's Charter
The Little Children's Prayer Book
The Soldier of Christ: Talks before Confirmation
Welcome! Holy Communion Before and After

Tales of the Saints:

A Child's Book of Saints by William Canton
A Child's Book of Warriors by William Canton
Illustrated Life of the Blessed Virgin by Rev. B. Rohner, O.S.B.
Legends & Stories of Italy by Amy Steedman
Mary, Help of Christians by Rev. Bonaventure Hammer
The Book of Saints and Heroes by Lenora Lang
Saint Patrick: Apostle of Ireland
The Story of St. Elizabeth of Hungary by William Canton

Check our Website for more:

www.staugustineacademypress.com

Lightning Source UK Ltd.
Milton Keynes UK
UKOW01f0049230218

318363UK00001B/52/P